Mapping in the Modern World

MENTAL MAPS AND MAPPING THE MIND

Enzo George

Crabtree Publishing Company
www.crabtreebooks.com

I0799386

Crabtree Publishing Company
www.crabtreebooks.com
1-800-387-7650

Published in Canada
616 Welland Ave.
St. Catharines, ON
L2M 5V6

Published in the United States
PMB 59051
350 Fifth Ave. 59th Floor
New York, NY 10118

Published in 2017 by CRABTREE PUBLISHING COMPANY
All rights reserved. No part of this publication may be reproduced, stored in a retrieval system or be transmitted in any form or by any means, electronic, mechanical, photocopying, recording, or otherwise, without the prior written permission of the copyright owner.

Author: Enzo George

Managing Editor: Tim Cooke

Designer: Melissa Roskell

Cover Design: Katherine Berti

Picture Manager: Sophie Mortimer

Design Manager: Keith Davis

Editorial Director: Lindsey Lowe, Kathy Middleton

Editor: Janine Deschenes

Children's Publisher: Anne O'Daly

Proofreader: Ellen Rodger

Production coordinator and Prepress technician: Ken Wright

Print coordinator: Margaret Amy Salter

Produced by Brown Bear Books for Crabtree Publishing Company

Photo credits
Photographs (t=top, b=bottom, l=left, r=right, c=center)

Front Cover: All images from Shutterstock

Interior: BBC: 12t; BC Deeks: 8; Becky Cooper: 9; Tony Buzan: Mind Mapping for kids 16; Olafur Eliasson: 26; Library of Congress: 4; Madiha Sikander/Cabral Government Boys Primary School: 5; Minecraft: 25; National Institute of Heath: 19; Public Domain: C.J. Visscher – Gerritsz 28; Saul Steinberg Foundation: The New Yorker 7; E. H. Shepard: 1, 23; Scala Archives: MOMA 27; Shutterstock: Boris15 21, Kentoh 24, Moloksos 29b, Phovoir 13, Anna Zubkova 20; Steve-lovelace.com: 28; Courtesy the artist and Tanya Bonakdar Gallery, New York: 26; Thinglink: 16; Thinkstock: Pewara Nicropithak 29c, Ondine32 17; J. R. Tolkein: 29t; Daniel K. Wallingford: 6; West Virginia Mountaineers: www.wvugame.com: 15; Wikipedia: 14, 18; HYPERLINK "http://www.pendalouan.org" www.pendalouan.org: 11. All other photos, artwork and maps, Brown Bear Books.

Brown Bear Books has made every attempt to contact the copyright holder. If you have any information please contact licensing@brownbearbooks.co.uk

Library and Archives Canada Cataloguing in Publication

George, Enzo, author
Mental maps and mapping the mind / Enzo George.

(Mapping in the modern world)
Includes index.
Issued in print and electronic formats.
ISBN 978-0-7787-3237-2 (hardcover).--
ISBN 978-0-7787-3243-3 (softcover).--
ISBN 978-1-4271-1886-8 (HTML)

1. Geographical perception--Juvenile literature.
2. Cartography--Juvenile literature. I. Title.

G71.5.G47 2017 j912.01 C2016-907131-6
C2016-907132-4

Library of Congress Cataloging-in-Publication Data

CIP available at the Library of Congress

Printed in Canada/052017/TL20170327

Contents

MENTAL SPACES

Making any map depends on choices. The choices a cartographer makes often depend on their personal view of their homes, communities, and the world.

Most of the choices a cartographer makes depend on what he or she intends a map to be used for. But some choices also reflect the personality of the mapmaker. Everyone sees the world around them in a different way, depending on their experiences. They know some neighborhoods better than others, and are more interested in some locations and landmarks than others. For young people, places such as their homes, their school, or the football stadium might play a much larger role in their lives than locations such as office buildings or **landfill** sites. Car drivers might not be aware of, or interested in, walking routes.

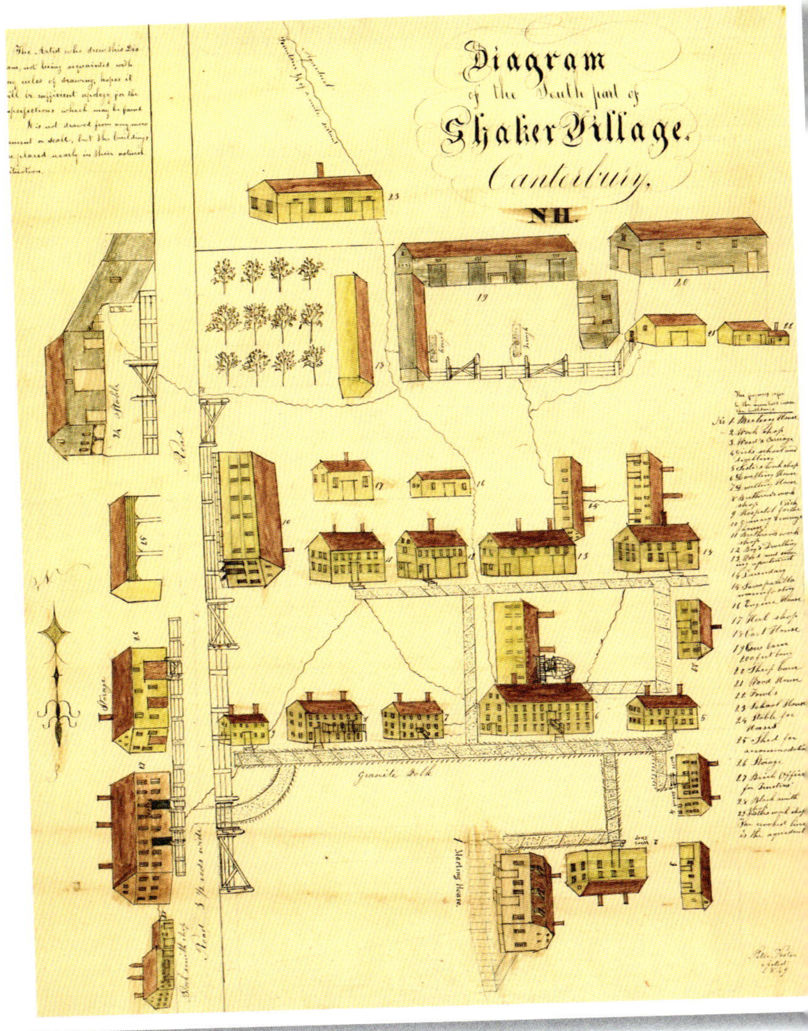

This map of a Shaker village in New Hampshire was drawn in 1849. It shows the buildings in the simple style familiar to the Shakers, a small Christian group that chose to live separate from the outside world.

A Child's-eye View

When schoolchildren mapped their neighborhood of Karachi, the capital of Sindh province in Pakistan, they included playgrounds that most adults would not notice. They showed the places where they play soccer and **cricket**—sometimes in spaces between buildings—as well as cafes and places to fly kites. They included the most brightly colored buildings.

The result is a map that shows how children see Karachi, which is one of the fastest-growing cities in the world. The map seems quite playful. It gives a glimpse into how children can find public spaces to use and repurpose for play and **recreation**.

A map of Lyari, a neigborhood of Karachi in Pakistan, drawn by schoolchildren in the town. It looks very different than an official map of the same neighborhood would look.

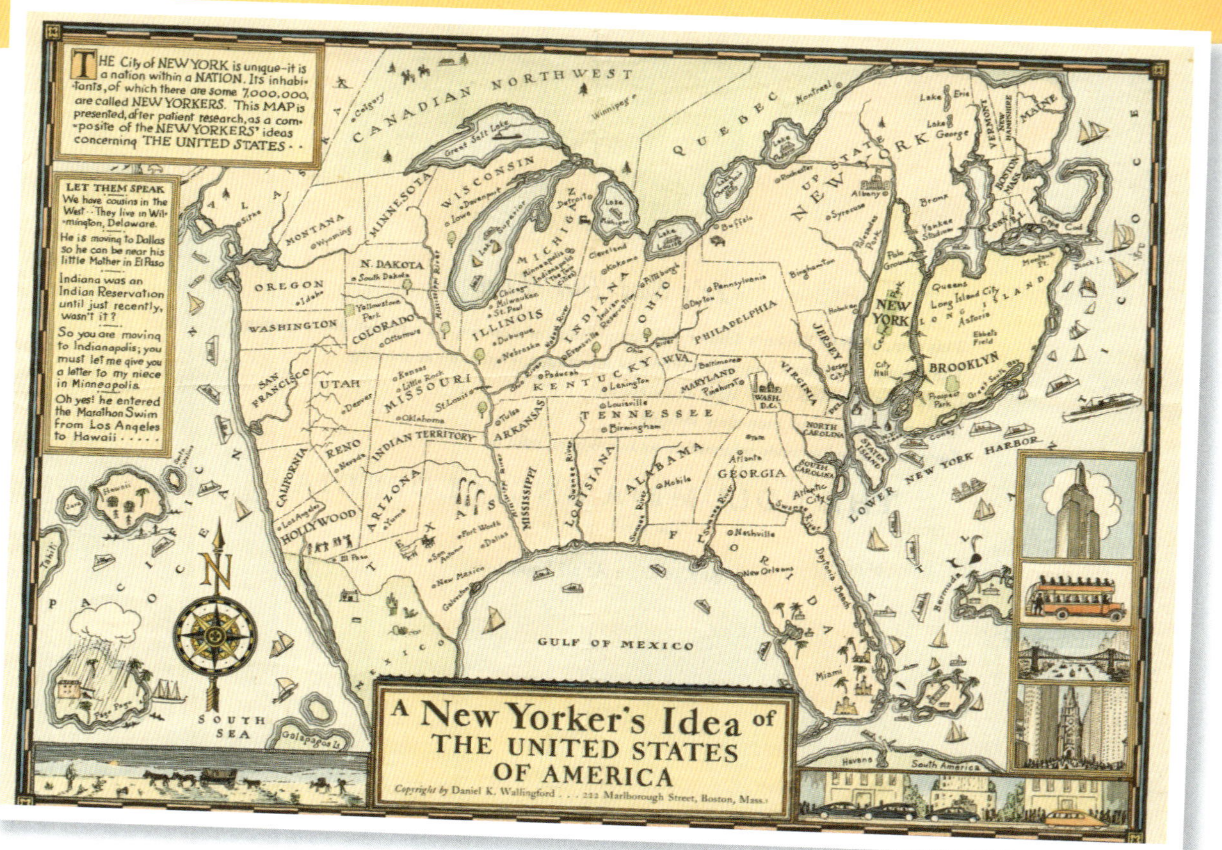

A Slanted View

Nearly all maps reflect the preferences and priorities of their creators, to some degree. Some cartographers choose to highlight these ideas in their maps. In the 1930s, a mapmaker named Daniel K. Wallingford drew what he called *A New Yorker's Idea of the United States of America*. He created a map of the United States that deliberately showed Brooklyn, Manhattan, and New York State as being huge. New York was drawn as the largest state, and the other states were far smaller than they really are.

Wallingford also included deliberate errors to poke fun at what he saw as New Yorkers' lack of geographical knowledge. For example, he places New Orleans and Nashville in Florida rather than in Louisiana and Tennessee, respectively. He divides California into three states, named California, Hollywood, and San Francisco.

What do you think Daniel Wallingford was trying to say about the people who lived in New York, based on this map?

The map was Wallingford's comment on the idea that people know more about the place they are from than about other places, and that they tend to see places closer to home as being more important than distant locations.

Looking at the World

A more famous map that depicted New Yorkers' views of the world was called *View of the World from 9th Avenue,* drawn by Saul Steinberg in 1976. At the bottom of the page was a detailed view of 9th and 10th Avenue in New York City. Beyond the Hudson River, the rest of the United States was a green strip with only a few places marked. Beyond the strip was the Pacific Ocean, with bumps on the horizon to show China, Japan, and Russia. Similar maps have been drawn for many of the world's cities. They all treat nearby areas as important and those farther away as unimportant.

Saul Steinberg's magazine cover is one of the most famous modern maps. It has been widely imitated.

In the Real World

A Novelty View

Saul Steinberg drew *A View of the World from 9th Avenue* for the cover of *The New Yorker* magazine. The map shows how people see nearby places as being important, but more distant places as being empty and unimportant. Steinberg's map reminds us that we put ourselves at the heart of our own world—and therefore of our own maps. The map has inspired many other drawings of biased "views from" cities and countries around the world.

Maps and Me

Your Own Memory Map

One way to explore the places that are important to you is to draw a memory map of your own neighborhood. The map can be simple, but you should try drawing it from memory. Don't try and fill in every detail. Instead, start by making a basic outline of the streets or roads. When you're happy with the outline map, try adding the buildings that play an important part in your life. Put them in the right locations on the map (you may need to adjust the positions of some of your streets). There may be a few or there may be many. You can try drawing and coloring them as you remember them to be. Then, compare your map to the map of a friend or classmate. What buildings did you both choose to show?

A memory map does not have to include every place in a town—just the ones that are important to you.

A similar observation of people's geographical attitudes lies behind maps of **stereotypes**. These are often humorous, because stereotypes are highly simplistic. For example, one map of the United States labels Wisconsin as "People Who Make Cheese," while in Wyoming the label is "Cowboys." However, these maps are not simply comments on the people of Wisconsin, Wyoming, or the other states. By placing labels on large areas, the maps show how broad and inaccurate the stereotypes are, because the labels could never accurately represent all of the people in the state. In that way, the maps also criticize the people who use these kinds of stereotypes.

Mapping the Senses

The way people think about places is not only about simple geography. It often also involves memories and emotions.

Did You Know?

The cartographer Kate McLean maps cities using smell. She walks the city streets making notes of what she smells, and where. She then uses colors to map them. She says that smell helps people to react to places on a more emotional level.

Some mapmakers have tried mapping locations by using smells and noises. They say these senses are closely linked to our feelings and memories, so the maps reflect how people really feel about particular places.

The artist Becky Cooper is interested in people's attitudes toward places. She hands out blank maps of Mahattan Island to New Yorkers. Cooper asks people to complete the maps with whatever is important to them about New York. Some people draw complicated maps. Others simply highlight places where important events happened in their lives. One drew dozens of gloves and entitled the map "My Lost Gloves." In other maps, Manhattan was covered in forest or shaded in blocks of color, which are more **abstract** representations of peoples' feelings toward a place. For example, a block of yellow color might represent an area where a person had a happy experience.

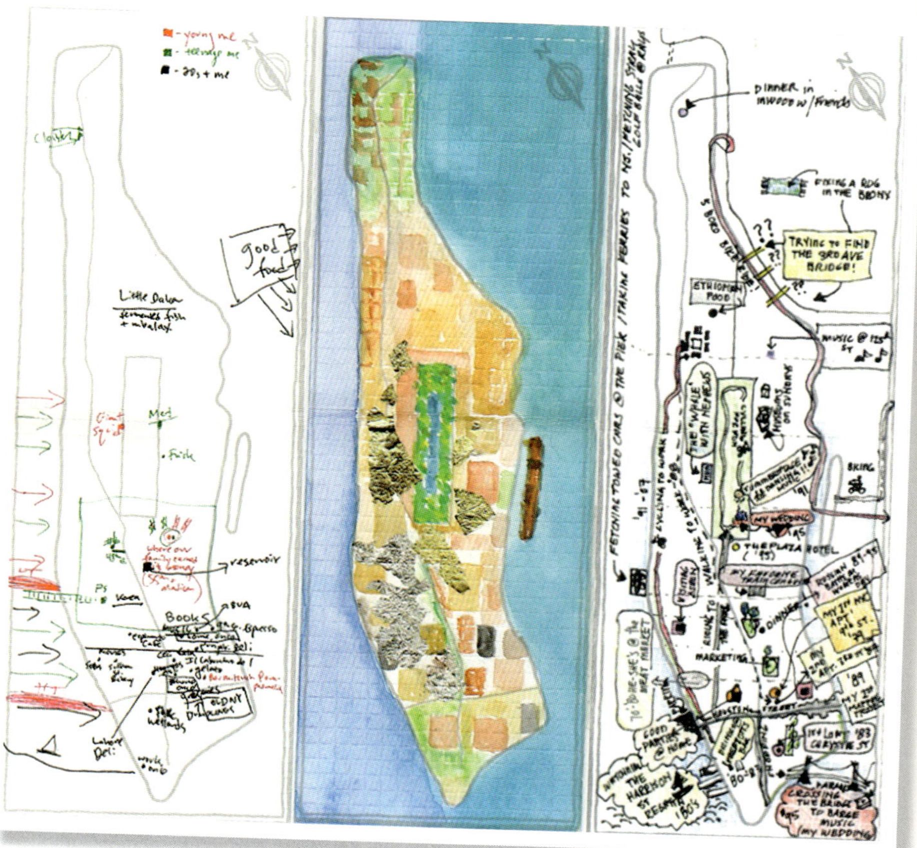

Becky Cooper gives people the same outline map of Manhattan to fill in. These examples show, from left to right: incidents from a person's life by decade; a map of the textures and colors of the city; a personal visual "diary" of the city.

YOUR GEOGRAPHIC FRAMEWORK

Everyone has their own ideas about geography. We see the world from our own point of view. This becomes clear when people make maps.

People's views on what is important vary widely. Think about your home. If you made a map of your bedroom from memory, you might pack it with detail. You could include any books or games, or what is on your desk or bedside table. If you tried to map the bedroom of another member of your family from memory, the map would probably lack detail. You are not as interested in it as you are in your own room, so you will probably leave more things out.

When we map the place where we live, we often only include important buildings and leave others out. This map has a simple key to explain what the symbols mean.

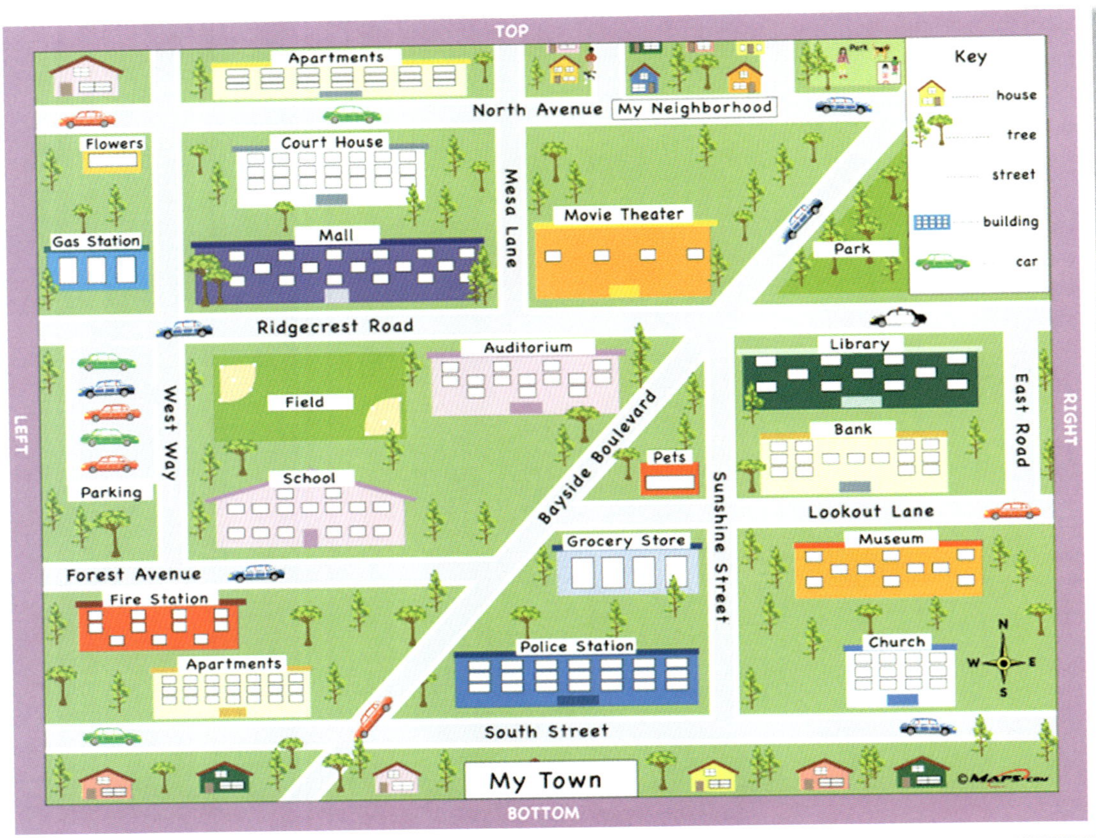

Mapping Neighborhoods

When children draw maps, they often show the buildings or places they know best as being larger than they actually are in relation to other places. The same is true of mapping on a larger scale. If some people mapped your town or neighborhood, they might not even notice the part of the local park where you meet your friends or the short-cut you take through the parking lot on the way to school. You would probably include features like this if you drew a map of your neighborhood, but you might not include an antique store that sells things you never need to buy, or a dead-end street you never take. How we **interpret** the world around us is our geographic framework. It often shapes the way that maps are created.

Some mapmakers use a painted style that combines the layout of a map with simple **3D** images of buildings, such as this map of a YMCA summer camp in Michigan.

In the Real World

Follow the Cats

Have you ever imagined how a pet might see the world? In 2013, British researchers tried to find out by tracking the movements of pet cats during the night. They attached **GPS** tracking devices to cats' collars. When they downloaded the data, they plotted each cat's movements on a map. By tracking a number of cats in the same neighborhood, researchers discovered that cats have fixed **territories** that they explore. Some cats travel up to 600 feet (182 m) away from home. When territories overlap, cats avoid confrontation by visiting at different times. If they do meet a rival, they fight to drive them away.

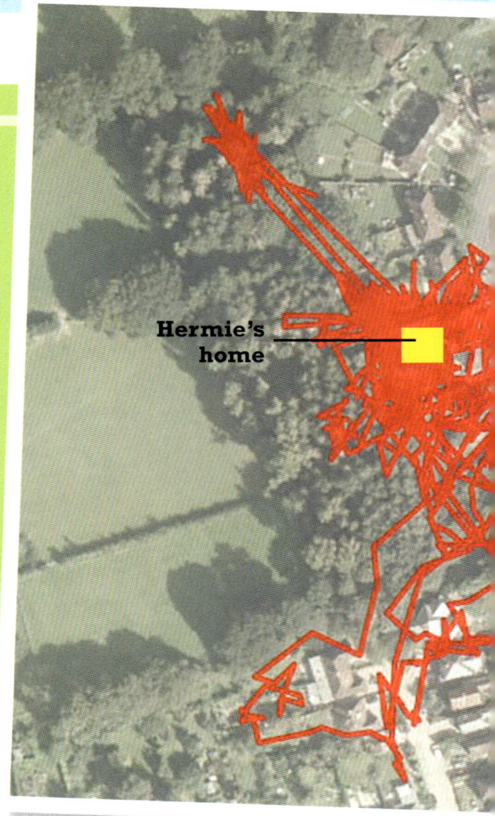

This map records the movements of a black shorthair cat called Hermie. Hermie's wandering covered a territory of 8 acres (3.3 ha).

Mapping Changes

Our geographic framework is unique to each of us. It also changes over time. Think about when you were younger. What places were important to you? Perhaps you often visited with your grandparents, so you remember the towns or streets where they lived. Perhaps you went to the same summer camp for a few years. As you grow older, your friends may have changed or moved. You may now walk or ride your bike along different routes to see them.

Your Own Map

Try drawing a map of a journey that you make frequently. It could be your journey to school, for example, or the route you take to visit a friend or relative. Include any types of transportation that you use. You can also include features along the way, such as stores, signs, or office buildings you notice, the homes of people you know, and other places you visit, such as a church or restaurant.

Looking Back

Now try drawing a similar map of a route you used to take often but no longer take. Draw it from memory. What would you include? What would you leave out? Try printing a street map of your town or neighborhood from the Internet. Use colored pens to highlight places that mean something to you. Use one color for places that used to be important, and another for places that are now important to you. Choose a third color for places that have been important to you for your whole life. The map you create offers a new dimension–it shows time passing. What do the different colors on the map tell you about how your life has changed over time?

Maps and Me

Maps, Size, and Scale

The **scale** of a map is the relative size at which things appear compared with their real size. A scale of 1:100000, for example, means that 1 inch on the map represents 100,000 inches (8,333 feet or 1.58 miles) of actual distance. Most maps use a set scale throughout. When children draw maps, however, they tend to vary the scale.

Children usually draw places they know well much bigger than places they do not know so well.

In the Real World

War Maps

Specialized maps are drawn for soldiers to use in wartime. These maps can mean the difference between life and death, so they focus on useful information. In World War I (1914–1918), soldiers dug networks of **trenches** facing one another. Maps helped soldiers figure out safe routes to take, and helped commanders plan attacks on the enemy.

This map of British trenches in World War I marks in red the routes to be taken by troops moving up to the front line (1 and 4) and by wounded men being evacuated (2 and 3).

Choose your method

There are many ways to map any location. The best method depends partly on the purpose of the map. Imagine that you visit a large sports stadium. One map might help you and your family to find the way to a nearby parking lot, and then show you the best route to walk to the stadium.

Once you arrive at the stadium, you might need another map to show you which entrance to use, where your seat is located, and the location of the nearest bathrooms and food stands. This kind of map is sometimes printed on your game ticket. If you then wanted to make a map of what you were watching—a play in a football game, for example—you would need another type of map. It would show only the field, so you could mark the position of the players. Each example is a map of the same stadium, but they look different because they all have different purposes.

Did You Know?

Sports broadcasters and coaches use "heat maps" to show where players are most active on the field. Cameras track each player and map his or her location each second on a digital field. At the end of the game, the places with most hits "glow" red and yellow. Areas where the player has been less often are blue or green.

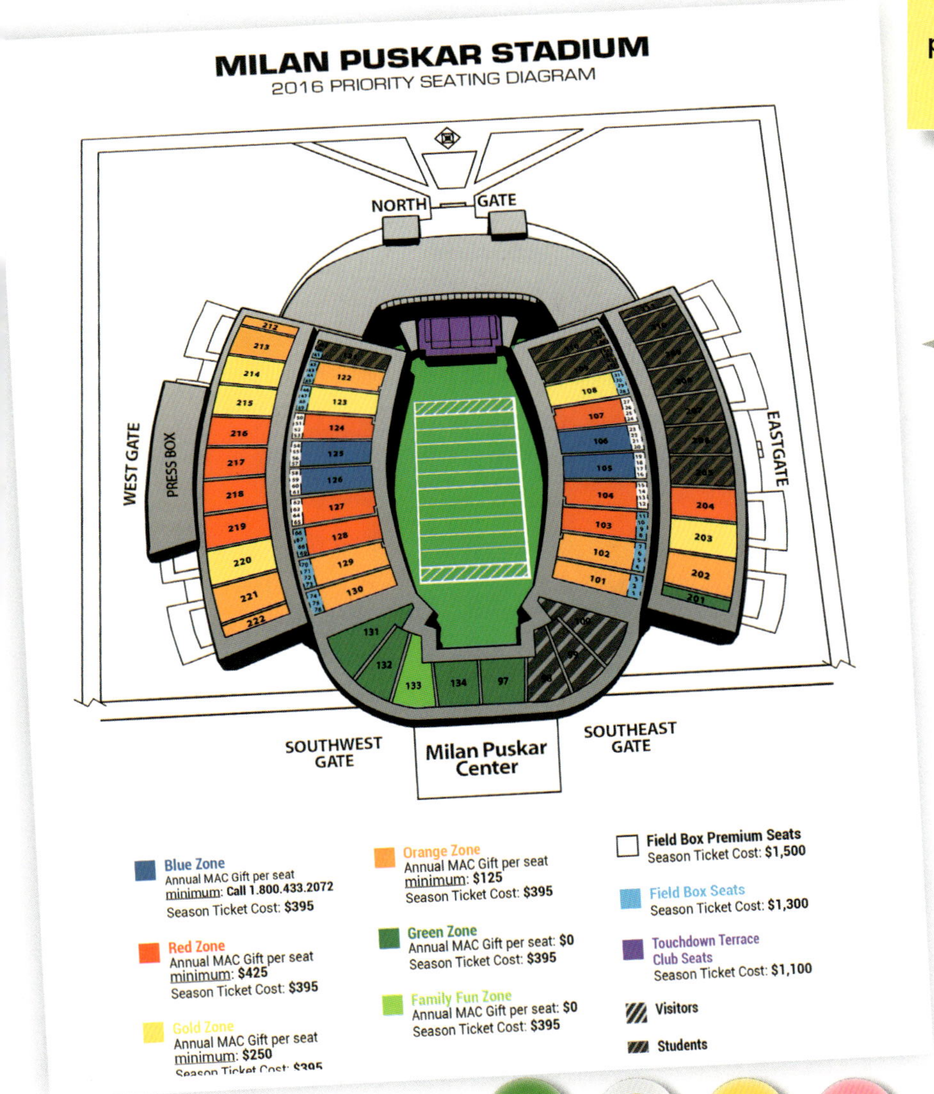

This map of Milan Puskar Stadium in West Virginia is colored to show the price of tickets in different parts of the stadium.

MAPPING THE MIND

Traditional maps show things as they physically relate to each other. Some maps, however, are not related to physical space at all. They map the imagination.

Mind maps are **graphic** maps that represent ideas and connections between them. They are a type of diagram that show how one idea or concept can lead to other ideas or concepts. The result often resembles a spider's web, with many branching connections.

Mind maps can be a useful way to record seemingly random ideas. By arranging the ideas in terms of their connections, mind maps may help people to recognize ideas that are or are not more important

This mind map reminds British children of the different topics they need to revise within subjects before taking exams.

People in a brainstorming session often write ideas on sticky notes to make them easy to see, organize, and move around.

than one another. Ideas can be **classified** and **visualized**. This helps people to organize their thoughts.

Brainstorming

Mind maps can be used in many different situations. One way they are used is to record real-time **brainstorming** sessions at work. In brainstorming sessions, participants call out ideas that are triggered by the conversation, while someone maps them on a blank poster or board. Finding new links can steer a discussion far away from the original idea–and possibly toward a more useful subject.

Mind maps can be used by students to arrange their notes in a way that makes them more helpful for reflection and revision.

Did You Know?

The term "mind map" was invented by a British psychologist named Tony Buzan in the 1970s. The idea of making graphic diagrams of ideas is far older, however. It dates back to ancient Greece.

Make a Mind Map

Mind maps are easy to make. Start by writing the topic of your mind map in the center of a large piece of paper. Then write any other ideas you think of around the center. You can fill the page if you like. When you are done, use colored lines to link ideas that are closely related. Link the most important ideas to the central topic, and then link those ideas to less important ideas. Use a different color for each set of links.

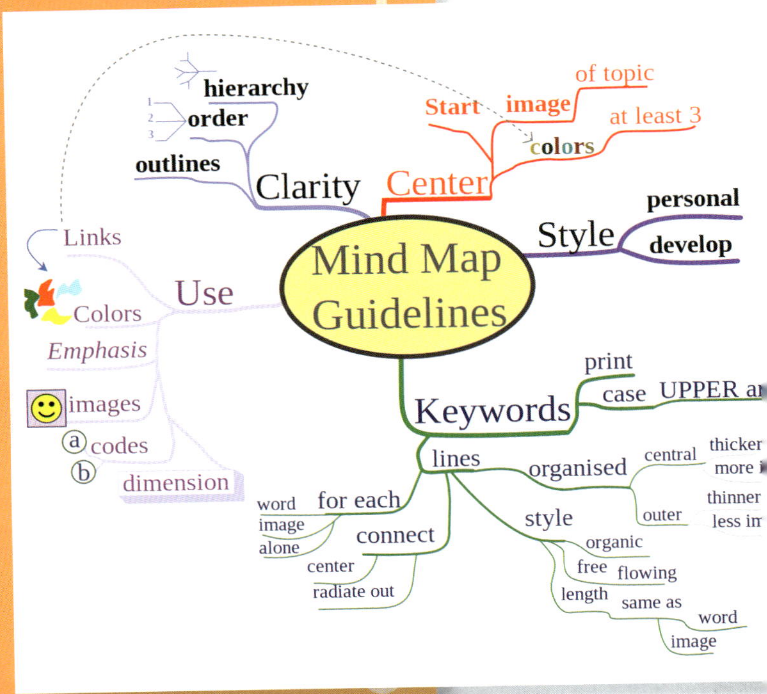

This is a mind map showing how to create mind maps. It gives advice such as using at least three different colors and using upper and lower case letters for words. You can use these guidelines to make a tidier version of your first mind map, which may look more messy.

Mind maps also help business people analyze their ideas when constructing a business plan. The graphic layout of mind maps helps people visualize their thoughts and figure out which ideas are central. Those that end up at the edges of the mind map may be less important.

Maps and Thinking

Different forms of mind maps, or graphic representations of ideas, have been used for many centuries. Recently, however, experts have been interested in the links between mind maps and the working of the human brain. Some experts believe that the brain processes information in much the same way as computers do. This means that the brain's workings may be represented as a kind of circuit, such as a diagram of an electrical **circuit board**.

An Ambitious Project

The Human Connectome Project is an international scientific project. Since 2010, it has been mapping the networks of the brain. The scientists working on the project believe that if the brain is a complex network, then its connections can be mapped. There are billions of individual cells called **neurons** in the brain. These make it difficult to map the brain in detail. Currently neurons can only be mapped in the broadest way, using **brain imaging** technology.

The colors in this map of the human brain indicate the direction that signals flow along the neurons.

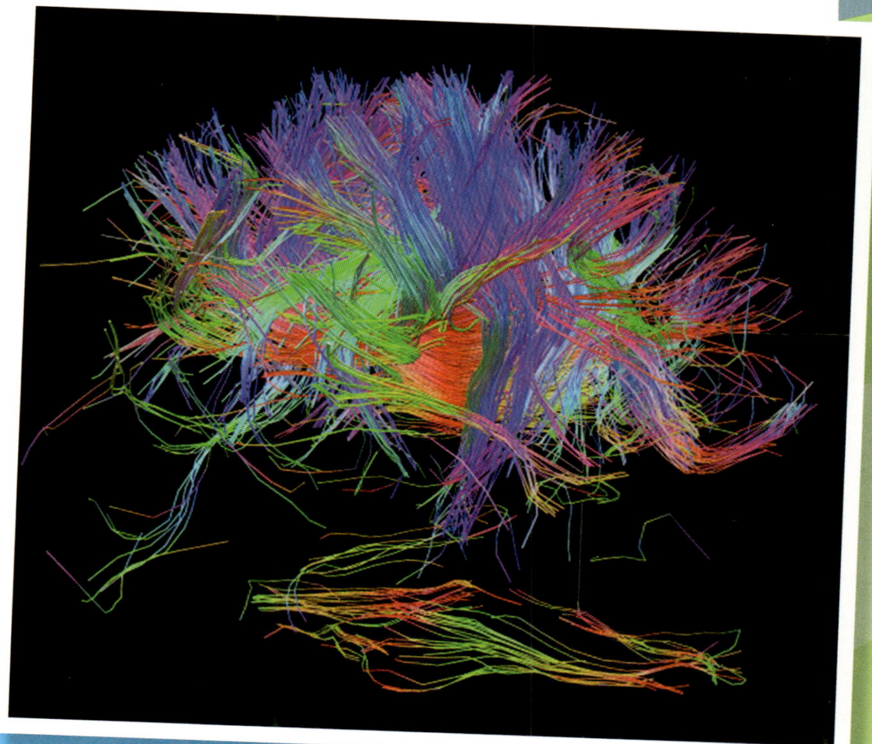

Breakthroughs

Mapping the Brain

The human brain is made up of neurons that are connected by pathways that carry tiny signals. The Human Connectome Project has set out to map the structure of the brain. It is an ambitious project, because experts have only a broad knowledge of how the brain works. Scientists hope that carefully mapping the connections will help them improve their understanding of the way humans think. They create images from brain scans. Eventually, they hope to create a digital map of the brain that will enable people to "fly" through its major pathways and explore the different regions that control different human functions.

Breakthroughs

Infographics

There are many types of infographics, which use diagrams to present factual information. **Infographics** first appeared in the 1600s and 1700s, and incorporated diagrams such as bar charts and pie charts. In the 1800s, infographics were used to present information such as the number of casualties in wartime. Modern infographics first appeared in Austria in the 1920s. The education board in Vienna developed a way of using simple graphics to present data for students.

Information on Paper

Mind maps are only one example of a type of diagram known as an infographic. Similar to maps, infographics lay out information visually for viewers to interpret. Infographics often display idea and information in different sizes, to show things that are more (larger) and less (smaller) important. This is similar to the personal maps studied in this book, in which certain locations and features are emphasized. Infographics also have a **spatial** element, so in many ways they can be seen as a type of map.

This infographic contains a range of information about water and how much water people need to drink to be healthy.

Mapping Text

A word map is an arrangement of the words people use on a topic, such as the words used in a speech or on their social media accounts. The text is usually analyzed by a computer program, and the words are fitted together in a "map." Words that appear most frequently are printed larger, and those that are used least frequently are printed smaller. Other words are sized according to how often they appear. The relative sizes of the words give an impression of what the speaker thinks is more or less important.

Word maps are a way to identify patterns in random data. In that way, they are like many modern maps that arrange data according to geography. Many people find it easier to understand information when it is displayed in a pattern. That is why maps and infographics play such an important part in our everyday lives.

Did You Know?

Word maps are also known as word clouds or tag clouds. The first word maps were produced in the 1990s, and became popular around 2005, when they were used to analyze content on social network sites such as Flickr.

This is a word map, or word cloud, of a text about changes in modern business and technology.

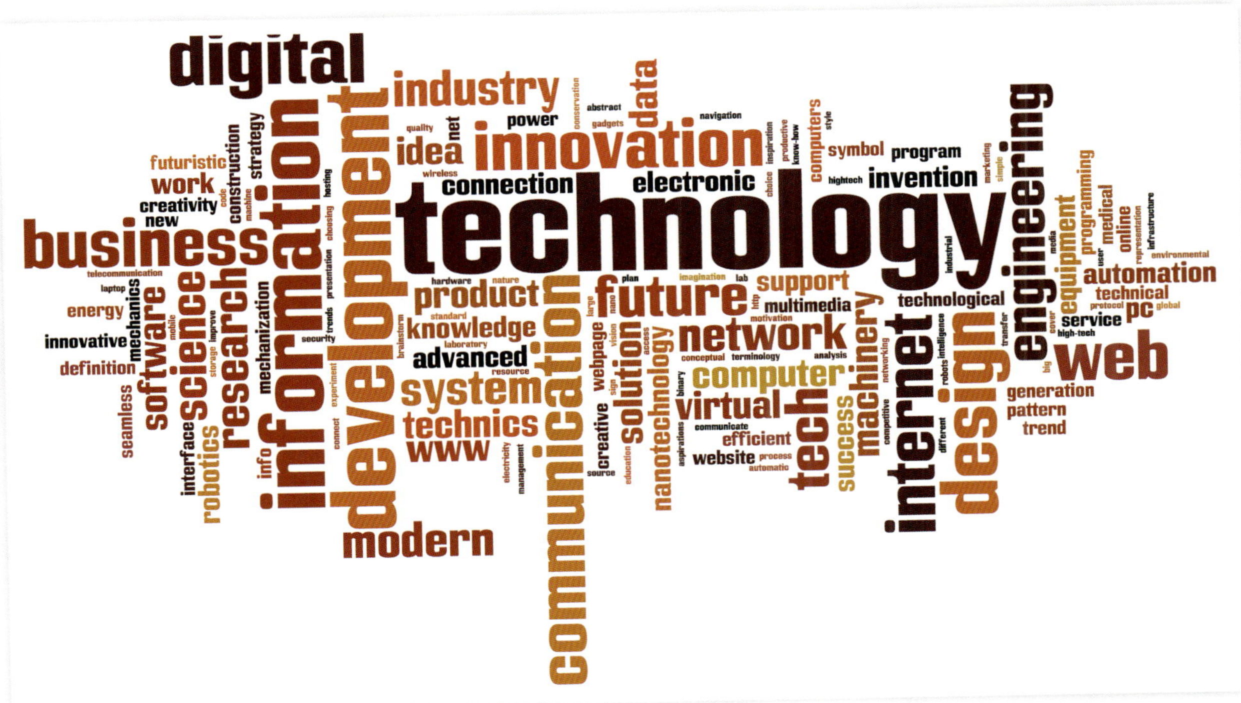

CREATIVE MAPPING

Many artists and writers have used maps in their paintings and books. These creators use maps to help people visualize imaginary worlds.

We tend to associate maps with real places. However, most people are also familiar with maps of imaginary places. For example, many schools and day-care centers have a carpet with a simple road map on it. Children enjoy drawing maps of imaginary towns and adding different buildings. In the past, some artists used their imaginations to draw maps of the world as it was described in the Bible—showing Adam and Eve in the Garden of Eden, for example.

The first maps many children come across show imaginary places where they can drive their toy cars.

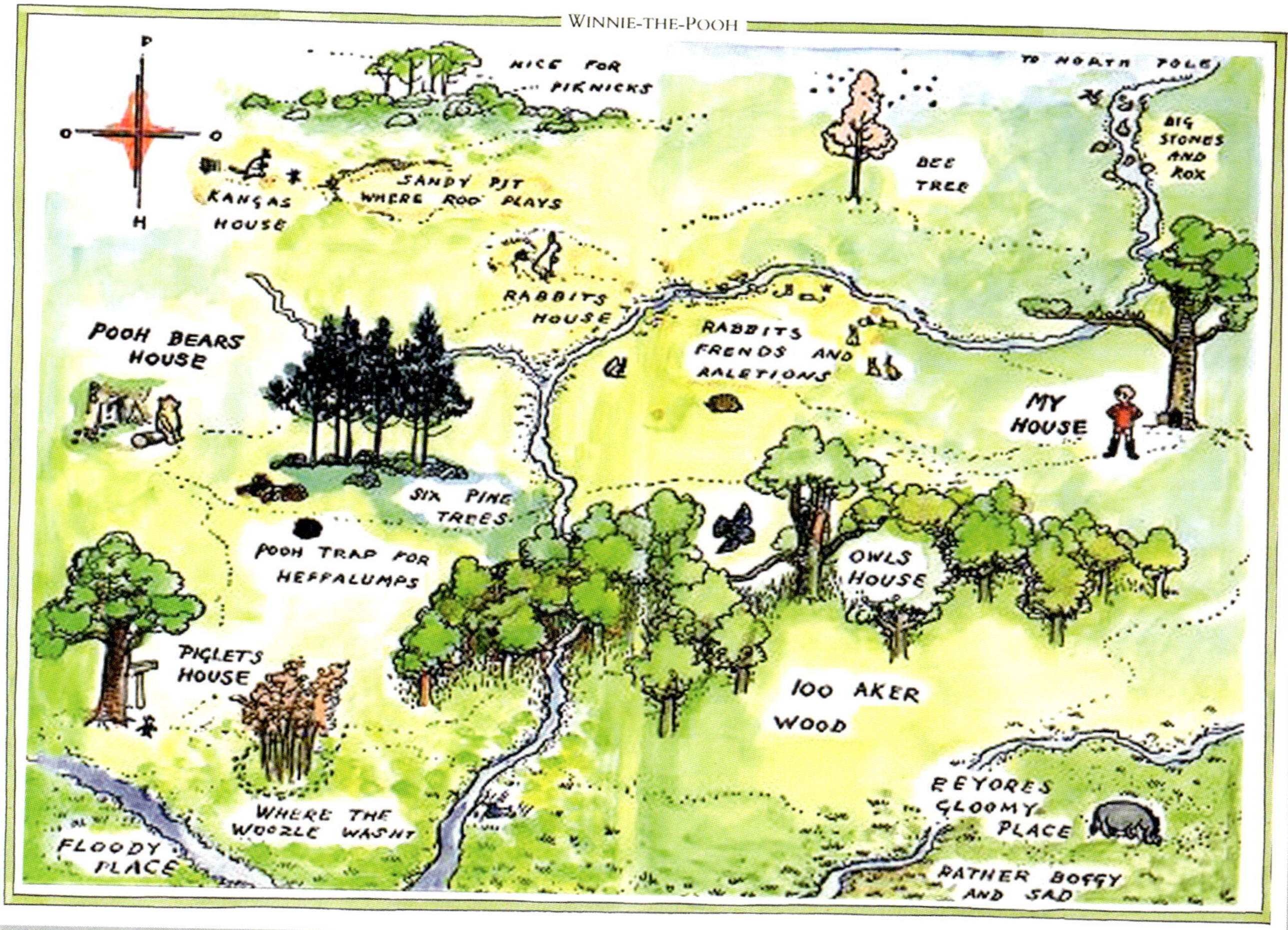

Hindu and Muslim artists have also produced maps and paintings of the universe as it is described in their holy books, the Vedas and the Quran.

Imaginary Worlds

Authors sometimes include maps in their novels. Maps help readers to visualize the whereabouts of characters in the book. For example, there are maps of classic children's books such as *The Wizard of Oz*. The famous movie and the books it is based on tells the story of a young girl who visits an imaginary land called Oz. The map shows her journey to meet the Wizard in the Emerald City.

British artist E. H. Shepard drew this map of the Hundred Acre Wood in 1972. It illustrates the fictional location for the adventures of a famous bear named Winnie-the-Pooh, written by A. A. Milne.

This map of a fictional city was created by adding detailed streets to an outline shape. This creates a crowded appearance, which makes it seem as though many people live there.

Maps and Me

Draw a Fictional World

A map is a good way to give a physical shape to an imaginary world. Decide what kind of map you want to draw: a street map, a map of a country, a map of a journey, or even a map of an entire world! Before you start, make a list of the things you need to include on your map. If you use symbols or colors, remember to include a key on your map. It might help to look at other maps to get some ideas. Take a large sheet of paper and some pencils—and get drawing!

Fantasy Maps

Maps are often connected with **fantasy** worlds. One of the most famous was the map of Middle Earth drawn by the son of the writer J. R. R. Tolkein. Middle Earth was the setting for Tolkein's novels, including *The Lord of the Rings* (1954). Christopher Tolkein carefully mapped all the main locations in his father's book.

Maps and Video Games

Many video games involve maps. Some are simple, such as the tracks in car-racing games—although these are sometimes very realistic depictions of real race circuits or the streets of real cities. Other video games are more complicated. **Simulation** games invite users to build a city or build a railroad. They use complex data analysis to predict what will happen in a particular set of circumstances. In the game SimCity, for example, residential neighborhoods become deserted if the player chooses to "build" polluting industrial factories right next door. Similar simulations are now used by government agencies to help **model** future city development.

Minecraft is another game based on geography. Users construct their own world as they play the game. The technology is being used by cartographers as a tool to make Minecraft maps of the real world.

Did You Know?

Christopher Tolkein drew the first map of Middle Earth in 1954. In 1969 his father, J. R. R. Tolkein, made notes on a version of the map in Elfish. Tolkein had made up the language to use in *The Lord of the Rings*.

This map is a guide to an adventure game called CobblStep City on Minecraft. Users can create and map their own worlds.

In the Real World

The Art of Maps

Many creative artists have made maps. They take advantage of the fact that some maps are instantly recognizable. By creating maps in unusual materials, an artist can make viewers look at maps more closely. By mapping familiar places in unfamiliar ways, artists who create these maps are able to prompt people to think about the maps they are looking at in new ways. Artists often use maps to make comments about subjects such as politics or identity.

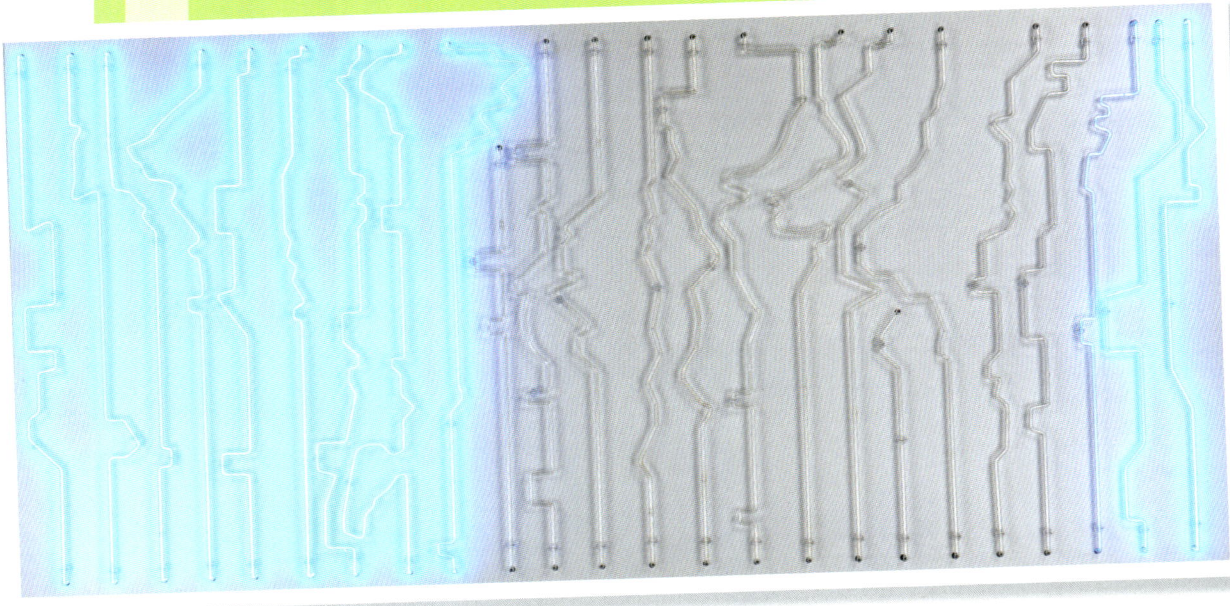

The artist Olafur Eliasson made this map of the lines that divide the world's time zones. The neon strips light up to show the part of the world that is in daylight at any time.

Artists and Maps

Some painters and visual artists draw maps of imaginary places, because they are skilled in illustrating the shapes and lines of maps. Others are more interested in investigating the part maps play in our lives. They use the methods of cartography, but apply them in unusual ways to explore how people think and feel about places.

A Map Experiment

Jasper Johns, an American artist, is an example of someone who used and created maps to explore how people think about place. In the 1960s, Johns was interested in symbols associated with the United States. He painted many versions of the US flag, for example, that represented ideas about the country. In 1961, Johns painted a map of the United States. He used bright colors that are not usually associated with maps, such as red and orange. Some states can be made out easily, but others are blurred. The names of the states are not always readable. Johns seems to be suggesting that the map is so recognizable that he does not have to paint it clearly. He said that the conventional map of the country was so familiar that people saw it without actually looking at it. Johns set out to make sure they looked at it more closely.

There are many ways to create an experimental map. This is the image of the United States created by Jasper Johns in 1961.

MAPS IN YOUR WORLD

Some maps are official and highly scientific. Other maps show information that is more personal to their maker. Maps can be a useful way to display and organize information about communities, thoughts, and wants or needs.

Although some maps require a lot of accuracy, such as a road map that shows people how to drive to different places, other maps can give a cartographer the freedom to display information in new ways. Maps such as these all reflect geography, but can approach the idea of place in different ways. Some depict fictional places. Tourist maps, meant to emphasize certain landmarks, leave out information or distort the scale, or size, of buildings and other features. Other maps reflect ideas about people or about maps themselves.

Look at the maps on these pages. What sort of map do you find most interesting? Using what you have learned in this book, how would you go about creating a personal map of your own neighborhood, or a mind map of the different ideas on a topic?

This map by the artist Steve Lovelace replaces the name of each state of the United States with the name of a corporation that Lovelace feels represents the state. His choice is usually a corporation based in that state. Try mapping your neighborhood using the names of the most important stores on each street.

Christopher Tolkein's fictional map of Middle Earth (above) visualized the setting for his father's books.

These images show a map of a floating market in Thailand (above); and a children's map showing the kinds of animals that live in different continents of the world (right).

Glossary

3D Describes a flat image that has an appearance of depth

abstract Describes art that does not try to represent something that exists in the physical world

brain imaging Technology such as scanners that create images of the brain

brainstorming A group discussion held to generate ideas

cartographer Someone who makes and studies maps

circuit board A small, thin board containing an electrical circuit, with components joined by pathways for electrical current

classified Something sorted into organized categories

cricket A bat-and-ball game played between two teams of eleven players

dissections Explorations of the inside of something by carefully cutting it open

fantasy Describes a type of story involving magic and adventure

fictional Existing only in an imagined story

digital Computerized

GPS Global Positioning System, a network of satellites used to provide location information

graphical Presented in a visual way by using graphs and other devices

imaginary Existing only in someone's imagination

infographic A visual representation of information or data

interpret To explain what one believes is the meaning of something

landfill Sites where waste is disposed of by being buried

model To use current data or information to predict how something will happen in the future

neurons Specialized nerve cells in the brain

recreation Acivities done for pleasure in one's spare time

scale The ratio between the real size of something and a representation of it

simulation Using a computer model to predict future scenarios

spatial Relating to space

stereotypes Widely held but oversimplified views of a person or group of people

territories Areas defended by an animal against others of the same species

trenches Long, narrow ditches dug into the ground as military defenses

visualized Formed a mental image of something

On the Web

www.nationalgeographic.com/kids-world-atlas/maps.html
National Geographic's site allows kids to create maps and explore the world and the people and places within it.

iknowwhereyourcatlives.com/about/
A site that plots the homes of pet cats around the world by using data freely available from the Internet.

www.nytimes.com/interactive/2013/02/17/magazine/mapping-manhattan.html?_r=0
View the different maps in, and read information about, the Mapping Manhattan project by Becky Cooper at this link.

https://www.template.net/design-templates/print/mind-map-template/
You can download templates for your own mind maps from this site.

Books

Berry, Jill K., and Linden McNeilly. *Map Art Lab: 52 Exciting Art Explorations in Mapmaking, Imagination, and Travel*. Quarry Books, 2014.

Boswell, Kelly. *Maps, Maps, Maps!* Displaying Information. Capstone Press, 2013.

Mizielińska, Aleksandra, and Daniel Mizieliński. *Maps*. Big Picture, 2013.

Panchyk, Richard. *Charting the World: Geography and Maps from Cave Paintings to GPS with 21 Activities.* Chicago Review, 2011.

Quinlan, Julia. *How to Draw a Map*. How to Use Maps. PowerKids Press, 2012.

Swindell, Salli Sue, and Nate Padavick. *Make Map Art: Creatively Illustrate Your World*. Chronicle Books, 2014.

Index